The

ONE-MINUTE
COUNSELOR™
for Parents

H. NORMAN WRIGHT

HARVEST HOUSE PUBLISHERS
EUGENE, OREGON

Cover by Dugan Design, Bloomington, Minnesota

THE ONE-MINUTE COUNSELOR™ FOR PARENTS
Copyright © 2015 H. Norman Wright
Published by Harvest House Publishers
Eugene, Oregon 97402
www.harvesthousepublishers.com

ISBN 978-0-7369-6104-2 (pbk.)
ISBN 978-0-7369-6105-9 (eBook)

Printed in the United States of America

15 16 17 18 19 20 21 22 23 / BP-JH / 10 9 8 7 6 5 4 3 2 1

Acceptance

Showing Approval

"What can I do to help my children accept who they are?
How can I help my kids avoid feelings of unworthiness?"

In my book *Raising Emotionally Healthy Kids* (written
with Gary J. Oliver), we offer these guidelines:

1. Ask God to help you be aware of how you feel
   about yourself. Many parents are hard on their
   kids because of their own unidentified and
   unresolved issues.

2. Ask God to help you appreciate the uniqueness of
   each one of your children and to be aware of their
   real needs.

3. Tell your children that you love them daily.
   Nothing defends against the attacks of shame
   or unworthiness like the security a child receives
   from the love and acceptance of his or her parents.

4. Affirm your children several times a day. Let them
   know that they are of infinite worth and value and
   are precious to you.

5. Give them quality time. This can be especially
   powerful after they have made a mistake or done
   something wrong.[1]

Two-Way Street?

"Someone suggested that I need to be accountable to my son. Is this correct?"

When we change and grow, we show our children that it is all right for them to change and grow. In fact, one of the best ways we can restructure our relationship with them as they mature is to build two-way accountability.

In two-way accountability, a dad would be willing to go to his teenage son and say, "Son, I'm working on not being anxious and, instead, committing everything to God in prayer. I'd like to report my progress to you each evening, and I'd like you to ask me occasionally how I'm doing. I'd also like you to suggest ways I can learn faster. And when you notice me getting anxious about something, please remind me to commit it to the Lord right away. Okay?"

When a parent initiates two-way accountability, he or she sets the stage for several things to happen: 1) teenagers will have a model for change that will help make change and growth easier to accomplish; 2) teenagers will have a model for voluntary accountability; 3) parent–teen communication will become more "adult to adult" rather than "adult to child."

Anger

When Everyone Gets Angry

"I get angry. My children get angry. Can you help?"

Every child gets angry. So does every parent. But children aren't born with control over their anger. They have to learn it.

Teach your children the cause of their anger. Usually anger is a secondary emotion caused by fear, hurt, or frustration. Ask your children why they're angry, and help them figure it out. Get them to talk about their anger in a positive way. If one of your children doesn't talk about his or her anger, you could say, "I can see you're upset. Would you like to talk about it?"

Help your children accept responsibility for their anger. God's Word says, "'In your anger, do not sin': Do not let the sun go down while you are still angry" (Ephesians 4:26). Give your children options for anger responses:

- "You can tell three of your friends how angry you are."
- "You can set a timer for 30 minutes, go to your room, and kick and yell until the buzzer sounds."
- "You can write a letter to God and tell Him how you feel."

Attitude

Adjustment Needed in Child

"My son defies me constantly. It's not just that he disobeys—
that I understand. His attitude really gets to me."

"Defiance is disobedience with an attitude." This adage
is true, and defiance usually pushes parental buttons.
Consider these questions and comments:

- Is this a constant behavior or now and then? If
  constant, change *your* way of communicating
  with your child until you find a way that works.

- Is your child reacting to the current problem or
  something else?

- You could say, "It sounds like something else is both-
  ering you." Take time to think about what you
  really want to say, how you could say it, what you
  would like to hear from me, and then we'll get
  together.

- This is a good time to model how to express being
  upset or angry in a positive manner. Remember it
  works better to lower your voice and tone rather
  than increase them. [2]

Keeping Kids Out of Trouble

"How can I help my adolescent children stay out of trouble without controlling them?"

Consider these suggestions:

1. Establish family discussion times. Keep them upbeat but meaningful.

2. Let your children know you want to hear what they have to say. There will be times when you *will not share* the same opinion or expertise on a subject. That's okay. To develop his thinking ability, he needs to explore ideas and beliefs. You may not agree with what he says; you can explain your opposing viewpoint.

3. Set limits on behavior but not on opinions.

4. Your teenager needs to be responsible for what he does. Don't let him blame others. He needs to accept the consequences for what he does.

5. Let your teenager make choices. Many conflicts can be defused if you approach your child with several options for a situation.

Creating a Cohesive Family

"I'd like to have our family get together regularly to share thoughts and ideas. We seem to go in so many directions that we're like strangers. Can something like this work?"

It can definitely work, but it will take effort on everyone's part. Some families hold meetings on a regular basis (once or twice a month). It will help to have a set time. Make your meetings 15 minutes to 45 minutes long. Let members know the estimated time length ahead of time. Future events or present concerns can be discussed.

Here are some guidelines for the meeting that will help make it go smoothly:

- Let each person know participation is important.

- Make sure everyone has opportunities to share and isn't cut off.

- Have each person share: "What's the best thing that's happened to you this week?" "What's the worst thing?"

- This is also a good time for a five-minute devotion, prayer requests, and a brief prayer.

Kids Too Stressed?

"My kids do too much. Some are stressed out—but not all of them. Why do some get stressed and others don't?"

Children who are able to cope with the stresses of life accept their strengths as well as their limitations. While they have a number of friends and respond well to their peers, they maintain their own identity. In contrast, peer-oriented children are less sure of themselves and often have a lower opinion of themselves. Kids who cope well are able to express their feelings. They share their hopes, anger, hurts, frustration, and joys.

If your children struggle with these things, sit down and listen while they share their feeling of disappointment or fear. The more often they share, the more comfortable they'll become with the process. Work with them to discover some alternatives to dealing with stress. Let them entertain anything from the ridiculous to the serious. Like some adults, certain children are not as affected as others by stresses of life.

Parents and "Someday"

"My daughter asked me to go somewhere with her, but I'm so busy. Is it all right to say no?"

Well, think about this: *Someday* when the kids are grown, things are going to be a lot different. You'll be able to park both cars neatly in just the right places.

> *Someday* when the kids are grown, the kitchen will be incredibly neat.
>
> *Someday* when the kids are grown, the electronics in our house will actually be available.
>
> *Someday* when the kids are grown, things are going to be a lot different. One by one they'll leave our nest, and the place will begin to resemble order and maybe even a touch of elegance. The phone will strangely be silent. The house will be quiet and calm...and lonely.
>
> And we won't like that at all. And we'll spend our time not looking forward to *Someday* but looking back to *Yesterday*.
>
> Paul said, "I have learned to be content in whatever circumstances I am" (Philippians 4:11 NASB).[3]

What Your Child Can Handle

"How can I tell if my child is getting too stressed out?"

Identify your child's general attitude toward stress:

1. "Things like this always happen to me."
2. He became unusually quiet and walked away.
3. "I never get what I want. Nobody cares about me."
4. "Boy, I'm disappointed." Then in a few seconds, "Maybe it'll work out the next time."
5. "This is no surprise. I was expecting something cruddy like this to happen."
6. "That makes me mad, but I didn't know about it. Is there anything I can do about it now?"
7. "That's not fair. It's just not fair!"
8. He didn't visibly react. He withdrew. He won't talk about it.

Now you can sit down with him and discuss the positive role of emotions and how to handle them in healthy ways.

Teaching Follow-Through

"My children don't do what I ask them to do. I'm giving one command after another. What else can I do?"

Here's an interesting approach to try.

> You can raise both the listening and compliance level of your child with one simple step—ask. Instead of ordering, "Go clean your room," ask, "Would you please go and clean your room?" The word to use is, "would," not "could.". . .No matter how you phrase it, note your tone.[4]

When you ask, avoid long explorations. Keep it short and avoid negative expressions. Have you said something like this? Fill in your answers.

"You're not listening to me."

- The last time I said this was
- The result was
- Another way I could phrase this is[5]

Chores

They're Good, But...

"I grew up doing chores. I expect my kids to do the same, but I'm not sure it's worth the hassle. It's easier to do the stuff myself. Any advice?"

In *How to Talk So Your Kids Will Listen*, I share these helpful suggestions:

> If your child comes to you and complains about his or her chores, consider what you would say:
>
> - "Tell me what you think you could be doing for chores."
>
> - "How much time a week do you think would be fair for doing chores?"
>
> - "Since we all have chores to do, are there certain ones you prefer?"
>
> - "Let's list everyone's chores for the week and then evaluate."
>
> - "You don't like us reminding you to do your chores. Think about it and then tell me your plan for reminding yourself."[6]

Avoiding Conflict

"I'm a 'limit' setter, but it feels like I'm giving commands much of the time. There's got to be a better way."

There is. Give your children choices.

Your child says something loud and unkind to you:

- *Fighting words:* "Don't you talk to me in that tone of voice!"
- *Thinking words:* "You sound upset. I'll be glad to listen when your voice is as soft as mine."

Your child is dawdling with her homework:

- *Fighting words:* "You get to work on your studying!"
- *Thinking words:* "Feel free to join us...when your studying is done."

Your child won't do his chores:

- *Fighting words:* "I want that lawn cut now!"
- *Thinking words:* "I'll take you to your soccer game as soon as the lawn is cut."[7]

Changing Your Approach

"I get frustrated with my kids at times. How do I change my communication responses from negative to nurturing?"

First, clearly identify the communication patterns you're currently employing. Begin recording your conversations at home. Then do this:

- Write out each of these verses about communication from the book of Proverbs on separate index cards: 10:19; 12:18; 14:29; 16:24; 17:9; 19:11; 29:20.

- On the back of each card write a statement describing how you see yourself complying with that verse. Make it specific and personal.

- Carry the cards with you for the next 30 days, and read each verse aloud several times a day.

Note how you change and how your child changes. When you employ toxic verbal weapons, such as critical and fault-finding comments, in your communication, you're standing against your children. But when your words are full of nurture and encouragement, you are standing with them.

Do's and Don'ts

"I try to give my daughter choices, but it doesn't work. Can you give me some examples?"

Here are some good ideas from Foster Cline and Jim Fay:

> Don't give too many choices at once. Two are sufficient, but if they can't choose one, there is a third. It's what you will decide for them. Most children would prefer the first two... Be sure your choices don't turn into threats. Don't say you have to choose my way or else. "You either wash the car or lose it for a week." That's a threat. It won't work in the long run. Here are *choices*:
>
> - "Would you mow the lawn or vacuum the downstairs so I have time to do the car?"
> - "Would you rather complete that school project tonight or Saturday morning?"
> - "Would you rather wash and iron your clothes or pay me to do it? I'm not that expensive."
>
> Be sure you're comfortable with the choices you offer.[8]

Giving Affirmations

"Someone suggested that we nurture our children. I'm not sure what that means. Any ideas?"

Nurturing messages are those that convey to your child something good about herself. These positive messages don't increase the child's value—she is already priceless in God's eyes. But nurturing messages increase your child's value *in her own eyes*, thus opening the door for learning, growth, maturity, and independence.

Nurturing shows that you believe in your child's capacity to learn, change, and grow. Nurturing shows that you are aware of the kind of picture you want your child to have of herself. Nurturing accentuates the positive.

It's easier for most parents to affirm positive behavior than to deal with negative behavior in a positive way. Continually remind yourself to convey nurturing affirmations and compliments:

- You treat your friends very nicely.

- Your schoolwork has really improved.

- You're a very special person to me.

Social Media and Technology

"I'm concerned about my kids and Facebook and other social media. My eight-year-old is more adept with technology than I am. Is this a danger zone?"

How can parents keep up with what their kids know about the Internet and social media?

- Put the computer in a room where people gather. Is your child trustworthy enough to have it in their room?

- Do your homework on what the Internet offers. Become knowledgeable.

- A mandatory rule is no contact with strangers— what no one gives out is name, address, phone number, credit card numbers.

- Set clear rules—Internet is OK for school reports. Permission is needed for other downloads.

- Set a time limit on its usage for email or playing games. No chat rooms—explain the reasons for this.[9]

Communication

Talking So They'll Listen

"My children just won't listen. And the more I tell them I need them to listen, the less they do. Help!"

Nancy Samalin has great suggestions:

> If [parents] want to be heard by their children, *they talk less*. The greater the amount of words that come out of the mouth, the more children's ears and mouths close...
>
> 1. Be sure to get your child's attention. Your child needs to listen to you with his or her eyes, since nonverbal communication accounts for 55 percent of a message.
> 2. Let your child know you're only going to be talking about 1 ½ minutes. Look at your watch and keep time.
> 3. Don't give a big answer to your child's little question.
> 4. Use the "one-word rule." That's right, say one word and no more.[10]

Verbal Abuse

"I don't want to talk abusively to my kids, but sometimes I just let my frustration rip."

Find someone you trust and start an "accountability" relationship. These questions will help you figure out and deal with your frustration:

- How do you feel about becoming frustrated? How do you feel about getting angry?

- When you're frustrated, do you want to be in control of your response or be spontaneous?

- When you're bothered by something your child does, how would you like to respond?

- Begin training yourself to delay your verbal and behavioral responses until your emotions have settled down.

- Your inner conversation—also called self-talk— is where your frustrations are either tamed or inflamed. Do you need to alter your self-talk?

- Keep a record of your progress by maintaining a "frustration diary."

Walking on Eggshells

"Sometimes it feels like I'm walking on eggshells. It doesn't take much for my kids and me to get into a hassle. What can I do? I feel like I'm tromping through an egg minefield."

If these land mines occur on a regular basis, you need to identify the following:

1. Where do the arguments, confrontations or power struggles occur?...If land mines occur in the kitchen, the teen's room or your bedroom, establish these areas as off-limits. Instead, establish a safe room—a neutral area such as a bathroom— for crucial discussions.

2. When do they occur? Some parents have said just before or after dinner, or just before they leave for work. To break this pattern, establish a rule in the house that says crucial issues cannot be discussed during the half-hour prior to or after dinner, or just before work.

3. One way to stay out of situations that lead to land mines is to establish clear rules.[11]

Preparing for the Dating Years

"We're at that place. Both my children are approaching the age of dating. How do I prepare them? How do I prepare myself?"

This is the time of life that strikes terror in the minds and hearts of parents. You can prepare by asking and discussing these questions:

1. What is the purpose of dating?

2. What qualities do you have to offer a dating partner?

3. What qualities do you want to see in a person you date?

4. What would you like to do on your dates? Where would you like to go? Are there some dating activities you feel you will not become involved in?

5. Do you want to date only Christians, non-Christians, or both? What is your reasoning?

6. How late should you be allowed to stay out?

Excessive or Not?

"I find myself constantly correcting my kids. I'm hard on me and hard on the kids. Isn't that the way to shape them into the people they need to become?"

Actually, one of the most destructive forms of verbal abuse is fault-finding. It's a form of judgment. Frequently a fault-finding parent is a perfectionist who holds the unrealistic expectation that his or her children ought to be perfect...

- Fault-finding deeply wounds the child.

- Fault-finding also wounds the parents.

- Fault-finding really doesn't change the child.

- Fault-finding is contagious.

- Fault-finding accentuates and reinforces the negative.

Scripture says, "Let us stop passing judgment on one another. Instead, make up your mind not to put any stumbling block or obstacle in the way of a brother or sister" (Romans 14:13).

Love and Correction

"What's a good way to correct or discipline my children? I don't want to put them down or discourage them, but some stuff needs to stop. Suggestions?"

Since we want to nurture them at all times, corrective messages need to be delivered in a positive, affirmative way. One way is to help them discover a better way or a different option regarding what you don't appreciate:

- Here is a way you can do this that you might like better.

- It sounds like it's hard for you to accept a compliment. Perhaps you need more practice accepting them, and I need more practice giving them.

- I'm not sure you heard what I said. Tell me what you heard, and then let me repeat what I said if you heard something different.

- That was a poor choice you made, but I have some good ideas you might want to consider.

- You're not paying attention. Something must be on your mind because you're usually so good at listening and thinking.

A Driving Contract

"My son is old enough to get his driver's license. What guidelines are reasonable?"

Here's a driving agreement one teenager signed with both her parents.

1. Before using either car, I will ask either my mom or dad if I can use the car and explain the purpose.

2. If I want to go somewhere for myself, my homework and piano practicing must have been completed thoroughly.

3. During the first six months of driving with my own driver's license, the radio will not be used while driving.

4. During the school year I will be allowed to drive to church on Wednesday night but cannot take anyone home without permission.

5. I will not allow anyone else to use the car under any circumstances.

6. I will be allowed up to thirty-five miles a week and after that must pay for any additional gas.

7. I will assist in driving for extended periods of time on our long vacations under all types of driving conditions.

8. I will not give rides to hitchhikers under any conditions, nor will I accept any ride if I should have any difficulty with the car.

9. I will either wash the car myself or have it done once every three weeks.

10. I will pay half the increase of the insurance costs, and in case of an accident, I will assume half the deductible cost.

11. I will not text nor use my cell phone while driving.[12]

Drinking and Drugs

"What do I say to my children about drugs? They're all around. Unfortunately, I used to use them."

Today everything seems to be available to kids, from alcohol to inhalants, from hardcore street drugs to prescription medications. At some point your children will be offered drugs and may have to fight peer pressure to say no.

Create an atmosphere where your kids can ask any question about any subject and you'll engage them in discussion—even drugs, drinking, and sex. Bring up these issues from time to time and discuss them in non-accusing ways. A major step is teaching them how to say no firmly.

Rule of thumb: *Children need rules and tools.* "Teaching about drugs and alcohol and how to resist peer pressure without being clear about do's and don'ts (tools but no rules) is evading your responsibility to make clear what is right and wrong. Stating do's and don'ts without teaching about drugs and how to resist them (rules but no tools) is like sending your child into a danger zone unprepared."[13]

When Your Child Is Using

"My son is doing drugs. What can I do?"

The plan you pursue must have the goal of abstinence. (If you're not sure your child is using drugs, I strongly recommend Bob Schroeder's *Help Kids Say No to Drugs and Drinking* and Steve Arterburn and Jim Burns' *Drug-Proof Your Kids*.)

When you discover drug use, you feel betrayed, angry at your child and the dealers, and probably struggle with feelings of failure. Sometimes talking with your child will work, but in many cases stronger intervention may be necessary.

In using intervention, you gather, with the help of a counselor, everyone you know who is aware of and dismayed by your child's involvement with drugs or alcohol. The intervention needs to be scheduled at a time when your child is least likely to be using drugs. During the intervention, ask your child to listen as each person presents evidence of the problem. If you recommend your child go for treatment and he refuses, the consequences need to be presented.

Depression in Children

"Sometimes I wonder if my child is just sad or if she is depressed. What are the indications of depression?"

Depression signs include:

- He might appear restless but doesn't become involved in activity.

- Withdrawal and inhibition. It's a listlessness. Your child may look bored or even appear to be ill.

- A depressed child may display physical symptoms.

- Many depressed children feel rejected and unloved. They withdraw from any situation that may disappoint them.

- She's negative about herself and everything in her life.

- A depressed child will show unusual levels of frustration and irritability.

- Some children will mask their feelings of despair by clowning around and acting foolish.

- Some children demonstrate drastic mood swings when depressed.[14]

Faith

Sharing Christ's Love

"I want to help my children grow in Christ. What's the best way to do this?"

Rosalind Rinker is known for her writings on conversational prayer. In one of her works she penned this meditation for parents to remind us all how to respond to our children.

1. *My child, I love you.*

    I love you unconditionally.
    I love you, good or bad, with no strings attached.
    I love you like this because I know all about you.
    I have known you ever since you were a child.
    I know what I can do for you.
    I know what I want to do for you.

2. *My child, I accept you.*

    I accept you just as you are.
    You don't need to change yourself. I'll do the
        changing when you're ready.
    I love you just as you are.
    Believe this, for I assure you it is true.

3. *My child, I care about you.*

> I care about every big or little thing which
>   happens to you. Believe this.
> I care enough to do something about it.
>   Remember this.
> I will help you when you need me. Ask me.
> I love you.
> I accept you.
> I care about you.

4. *My child, I forgive you.*

> I forgive you, and my forgiveness is complete.
> Not like humans who forgive but cannot forget.
> I love you. My arms are open with love.
> Please come here! Come here to me!
> I forgive you.
> Do not carry your guilt another moment.
> I carried it all for you on the cross.
> Believe this, it is true.[15]

Helping Children Cope

"Both my children (ages 5 and 11) are still afraid at night. How do I help them?"

Kindly address their fears and offer solutions. "Tonight you get to sleep in your own bed. If you want, I'll stay outside your door for a few minutes to make sure you're all settled and safe. Do you want me to do that?"[16]

Let them know that it's all right to be afraid. Help them understand that being afraid is normal and *temporary*. Have them share what they're afraid of and why. Just talking about it brings it into the open and makes it more manageable.

Give them response options. For instance, teach them a simple prayer that acknowledges God is with them all the time. Encourage them to pray it when they get scared. Try role-playing. Have them imagine being in their rooms and everything is safe. They wake up in the dark...and it's still safe.[17] If nightmares are repetitive, have your child mentally change the ending.

Read these Scriptures aloud before they turn out the light (or they can read them): Proverbs 3:6, 24-26; Psalm 4:8.

Fear

Kids and Worry

"My eight-year-old and fifteen-year-old have got a bad case of the worries. Any suggestions?"

Talk openly with your children about their worries. Discover what's causing it.

- Encourage your kids to keep track of their worries by making a list.

- Teach your kids simple, creative exercises for stopping stress. On one side of a 3 x 5 card they can write STOP in big letters. On the other side they can write Scriptures, such as Philippians 4:6-9. Have them carry the card with them. When worry or anxiety strikes, they take it out and read the word STOP. After that they turn the card over and read the Scripture. Saying the word STOP breaks the thought patterns and interrupts the impulse to worry. And reading God's promises becomes a positive substitute for worry.

- Read these Scriptures to them regularly: Matthew 6:25-34; 1 Peter 5:7; Isaiah 26:3.

Separation Anxiety

"My young children get upset when I leave. I reassure them I'll be back, but it doesn't always work. Now what?"

Separation anxiety is more intense when a parent goes away for a long time. A brief separation isn't usually a major problem if parents handle it wisely.

1. *Take it slowly.* Take time to reassure your children before you leave and explain when you will return. It helps to develop rituals for separating.

2. *Take time to familiarize your kids with their environment and caregiver.* If at all possible, spend some time with your kids in the new setting a few days in advance of the separation.

3. *Make your reunion a fun time.* Develop "hello" rituals—a long hug and a brief talk about the time you've been gone. This gives your kids a routine to look forward to.

4. *Don't sneak away and don't be angry if your kids protest your departure.*

5. *Don't be irregular about picking up your kids.*

When Children Are Afraid

"How can I help my children overcome fear?"

Anticipate the fearful situations and address them in advance. This helps your children know what to do.

- Some parents believe that forcing their kids to face their fears is the best approach to take. Unfortunately, it tends to make the problem worse.

- Shaming, ridiculing, or punishing your child only aggravates his fears.

- Overprotecting your child keeps her from growing emotionally and learning to deal with fears.

- The best way to begin overcoming a fear is to face it a little at a time, starting from a safe distance.

- Make a plan for overcoming fear. In reducing any fear, it's important to think up several approaches.

- Memorizing God's Word is a positive step toward eliminating fears. Help your child memorize these passages from the Amplified Bible: Isaiah 41:10; 26:3; 43:1-3.

Apologizing and Forgiving

"I want my kids to be willing to apologize when they're in the wrong and forgive when someone else is in the wrong. How do I teach this?"

When it comes to apologizing, teaching the form is easy, but getting children to be sincere can be difficult. At first, don't insist they sound sincere. What's important is for them to learn when they're wrong and to admit what they did was wrong. Then comes the apology. Later on, when everyone has calmed down, you can address the actual behavior and the effects of an honest and sincere apology.

The best way to teach your child to apologize is to model it for them when you're in the wrong. Your children will appreciate your honesty and come to understand the importance and power of a sincere apology:

"You know, I was wrong to scold you in front of your friends. That must have been hard for you. I won't do that again. Will you forgive me?"

"I'm sorry that I didn't listen to what you were saying. I'll pay more attention next time."

Grant Gradually

"My son is fourteen, and he wants freedom. We want him to have freedom too. But there are still necessary rules."

Gradually granting your child more freedom and control as he matures is healthy and prepares him for adulthood. It's a teen's nature to want more…and more.

- We want you home by _____. Your teen will ask, "Why do I have to have a curfew?" Perhaps you want your teen to get enough sleep, so he or she is rested for the next day. Perhaps they broke your trust and they need to rebuild it… When you respond, don't say, "Hey, we set the rules here in this house!"…

- We need to know where you are and who you're with.

- We need to know when you're leaving for home.

- You can call us at any time of the night, and we'll come get you.[18]

Peer Pressure

"Next year our kids hit middle school and high school. What should we do to help them deal with peer pressure?"

Here are some thoughts to consider.

- Kids build their self-image by conforming. This can be good and bad. For some kids, going along with the trends of others helps them discover more about themselves. They discover insights into who they are, what they like and don't like, and what they really want.

- Don't overreact to some of the fads.

- Teach your child how to evaluate and how to properly say no as well as yes. "I'm just not interested" or "That's not for me."

- Encourage your child to feel good about not going along with the crowd. "You can decide what's best for you. Ask yourself, 'Do I want to be known for that behavior?'"[19]

- Have them memorize Proverbs 4:23 and Romans 12:2.

For Children

"I have a plan for my children's lives so they'll turn out right. Is this okay?"

Have you ever seen architects at work? They go to their drawing boards and, in very intricate detail, design the end product. Many parents today are like architects. They mentally design all aspects of their children, including the end product. They believe they are responsible for how their children's lives turn out. They have a clear and definite picture of what they want their children to become. They carefully guide and control their children's activities, choices, and relationships.

All good parents have a tendency to want to mold their children to match the design we desire for their lives. If their unique tendencies threaten our plans, we try to make their differences disappear. That puts us in conflict with God, who wants our children to be created in *His* image.

Appreciating their uniqueness greatly reduces parental frustration!

For Parents

"I'm not doing the best job parenting. I feel like I'm drifting. I think I need a course correction."

My first questions are, "Who do you want your children to become?" "What are the character qualities you want them to develop?" "Do you have blueprints you're following?" It helps to use a tailor-made plan for each child that contains built-in flexibility. Remember, your children may elect not to go along with your plan.

1. *Identify in writing what you want your parenting pattern to become and what you want to see happen in your child.* This step works best when both you and your spouse are united in a team effort.

2. *Communicate your new plan to your child.* Sit down with your child and inform her about your goal for her life. Explain as much as she is capable of comprehending about how she can expect you to respond to her under this new approach.

3. *Implement your plan.* To help you get started, read your new written plan aloud every morning and afternoon for 30 days.

Grief

Children and Personal Loss

"We've had some losses in our family. How do I help my children handle them?"

It's natural to want to guard our children against hurts and sorrows. We do this in two main ways. First, we say, "Don't feel bad. At least you have other friends (toys, grandparents, and so forth)." At this point we're comparing losses to minimize feelings. But comparison does more harm than good.

Second, we tend to edit the story of what has occurred and focus on anticipated benefits so our children won't feel so bad or be so sad. Minimizing the impact of a loss can leave a child feeling confused, misunderstood, and hesitant to talk.

Instead, say things that *affirm* legitimate feelings:

- "You must be feeling pretty sad right now. You really loved your grandma, didn't you?"

- "I sense you had high expectations for your performance."

We want to encourage our children to experience the full range of emotions.

How Do Children Grieve?

"Do children grieve? Their thinking is so different. When their grandpa died, one minute our kids were sad and crying, and five minutes later they were playing and laughing."

Children are the forgotten grievers in our country. Adults receive the attention, and children are left out of the equation. Here are some unique features of a child's grief:

- It comes out in brief intense episodes in the middle of everyday life.

- It can be put aside easier. One question may be about a grandfather's death and the next response is about a doll.

- Grief is expressed in actions. They're limited in their verbal expression.

- They often postpone grief…or parts of it, so it can last into adulthood.

- Children grieve differently from adults. Instead of experiencing ongoing intense distress, many children are likely at first to deny death and then grieve intermittently for years. [20]

When a Pet Dies

"We lost our beloved dog, who grew up with our children, who are now ages 6 and 9. How can I help them cope?"

This could be your children's first time dealing with illness and death. Here are some do's and don'ts.

- *Face your own grief*: This death could be a double burden for you.

- *Don't fudge the truth*. Be honest about the death or impending death.

- *Make room for questions—all of them*. Young children will ask and ask and ask.

- *Don't neglect goodbyes in word and deed*. This is a time for the entire family to talk about their companion who died.

  - "Let's talk about our cat that died."

  - "What do you wish you would have said to [Kitty]?"

  - "Did [Kitty] ever talk to you? What did she say?"

When It's Your Child

"One of my kids has a serious illness. What do I need to be aware of for my child and family?"

Much of your life will now revolve around your child with the illness and the effects of that sickness: special meals, cancelled vacations, a change in living conditions, trips to the doctor, searches for information and help. Your child with the illness will experience loss, you will experience loss, and so will any other members of the household. A child's illness will also impact your marriage and your job.

You'll need to face your emerging fears as soon as possible. You're probably afraid your child will suffer, afraid your child won't recover, afraid you can't handle the responsibility, and afraid your child might die (even if nothing has been said about this possibility).

And what about all the questions you'll get from family, extended family, friends, and church members about your child's condition? You'll need to answer them even though you may not have digested all the information yourself.

Establishing Boundaries

"I bet I've said the word 'no' to my kids thousands of times. I wonder what I could use instead. Any suggestions?"

The word "no" is a fighting word. It's a challenge to kids. Parents set limits and dare their children to disregard them. Saying "no" usually prompts an "Oh, yeah" response. Have you ever wondered why this is one of the first words a child learns?

> What a child hears in place of "No" is "Maybe" or "Yes," and they'll push us.
>
> Replace "no" with "yes." It's not that hard.
>
> - "No, you can't go to Jimmy's until you practice your clarinet." Instead, "Yes, you can go to Jimmy's after you practice."
> - "No, you can't play computer games until the dog yard is cleaned thoroughly and both dogs fed and watered" to "Yes, you can play computer games as soon as the dog yard is cleaned thoroughly and both dogs are fed and watered."[21]

Your Child's Future Spouse

"I'm concerned about who my child dates and the one he'll eventually choose to marry. What can I do?"

Many parents become anxious about this—especially when their children reach the dating years and their choices of potential partners appear to lack wisdom. Some parents begin praying for their son or daughter's future partner when their child is young. Here's a prayer you can use as a guide.

> Our heavenly Father, we thank You for the gift of our children. When it's time for them to find their life partners, we ask even now for the Holy Spirit to be their guide. We pray that the ones You lead into our children's lives have hearts of love for You, personal relationships with Jesus, and a commitment to live according to Your holy Word.
>
> May we as parents never be a hindrance to the growth of their marriages. We also pray that our children will be all they need to be as loving spouses.

Teaching Financial Savvy

"My kids think we're made of money. They want and want and want. I need some help for them and for me."

There are several things you can do.

- *Give an allowance.* Don't pay them for family chores; those are separate. This is money for them to live on for a week. This is all they get.

- *Don't insist that children save their allowance.* How can they learn to handle money if they stash their allowance in a shoebox at the back of their closets to save for when they get big? Kids must go through their own economic depression—wasting money and then not having any when they need it—to learn about money. [22]

- *Let them spend their money as they want.* And when it's gone…it's gone. Don't give them any more unless they want to take out a loan for something—and you're willing to do that. If you do, make sure there's a due date for the repayment of the loan. Yes—*a repayment.* Use a promissory note you both sign.

Some Don'ts

"We didn't grow up in healthy families. How can we make sure our family is different?"

It's easier to suggest what to avoid.

Verbal and emotional abuse. Yelling at your kids or making disparaging remarks about them. Also:

- Ignoring a child (not listening or responding).
- Giving a child negative choices only. "Either eat all your dinner or you will get a spanking."
- Constantly projecting blame onto a child.
- Overprotecting a child.
- Giving double messages. "Yes, I love you. Now, don't bother me!"

Rigidity. Unbending rules, super-strict family life-style, and legalistic belief system.

Repression. Overcontrolling or repressing emotions.

Triangulation. Parents using child as a go-between.

What's Effective, What's Not

"We hear about permissive, restrictive, neglectful, and authoritarian parenting styles. Which is best?"

I like what Jack and Judith Bolswick say:

> Two factors...have emerged as the most important elements in good parenting. The term *parental control* means that you, as a parent, actively provide guidelines, set limits, direct and redirect your child's behavior in some desired directing. The term *parental support* refers to the affirmation, encouragement and general support that you give to assure your children that they are accepted and cared for.
>
> Some parents are great at teaching right behavior but not so good at following through in their own lives...
>
> On the other hand, parents who model right behavior but never provide explanations and good reasons for the values and beliefs they hold are also lacking appropriate skills.
>
> It is important that [parents take] time to give the *whys* of the behavior they expect.[23]

When Parents Are Exhausted

"Some days I'm just so exhausted. How can I maintain calm to handle everything?"

Fatigue, weariness, exhaustion. These seem to be the built-in companions of parenthood. In fact, whenever a baby is born you bring these uninvited guests home from the hospital! *Every* parent feels completely worn out periodically. That's normal.

Some days you may want to wave a white flag of surrender and say, "I give up! I need someone else to take over." Some days you may get weary of waiting. Some days you may get weary because of criticism. *Weariness is a sign that you need to rest and refresh.* If you don't, you could move easily into the malady called burnout. Yes, there is such a thing as "parental burnout"! And you won't recover very quickly from it.

The more you try to carry everything alone, the more exhausted you'll be. The more you give to Jesus through prayer, the stronger you'll feel. So let God's Word energize you. Draw strength from God's promises and love. Take time to regularly read Isaiah 40:28-31 and Matthew 11:28.

Personality

An Extrovert Child

"My child talks and talks. She seems to know everyone at school. Her cell phone is always on. Are all kids like this?"

Welcome to the world of the extrovert!

- Extroverts tend to talk first, think later, and don't know what they'll say until they hear themselves saying it.

- They tend to speak louder, faster, and are more animated. They brainstorm out loud for the whole world to hear.

- They know a lot of people and count many of them among their "close friends."

- They don't mind reading or having a conversation while the TV or radio is on.

- They are approachable and easily engaged by friends and strangers alike.

- Extroverts need people around to recharge.

- Sometimes they can exaggerate; they share openly; they don't keep secrets.

- They like going to social events and talk with as many people as possible.

- They find listening more difficult than talking; they don't like to give up the limelight.

- They may think they've done a good job, but they won't believe it until they hear it from someone else. They have a high need for verbal affirmation. They may ask you again and again, "What do you think?" "Do you like this?" "Does this look good?"

Let your extrovert be an extrovert. This may be difficult, especially if you're more of an introvert yourself. But if you fight your child's basic personality preference by trying to remake him in your own image, you'll frustrate yourself and wound your child.

Extroverts have a high need for affirmation and compliments. He needs them daily. If they aren't there, he'll go looking for them.

An Introvert Child

"My child is quiet and doesn't respond to my questions instantly. And he doesn't have a lot of friends like my other children. Am I missing something about him?"

It sounds like this child is an introvert. People are born with a personality bent. They're actually a blending of an introvert and extrovert, but one is usually more dominant. Consider the characteristics of an introvert:

- They rehearse things before saying them, and some prefer that others would do the same; they often respond with "I'll have to think about that" or "Let me tell you later." Introverts need to think to speak.

- They enjoy the peace and quiet of having time to themselves; they find their private time too easily invaded.

- Introverts are like a rechargeable battery. They need to stop expending energy and rest in order to recharge.

- They are perceived as "great listeners" but feel that others take advantage of them.

- They tend to understate points.

- Sometimes others think they're not interested or tuned in because they're quiet.

- They like to share special occasions with just one other person or perhaps a few close friends. Large family gatherings can be draining.

- They like stating their thoughts or feelings without interruption.

- They get suspicious if people are too complimentary.

- They need less verbal feedback and prefer that it be given in private.

Support him when he faces a threatening group environment, such as new classes and teachers on the first day of school.

When you talk with your introvert child, do so in a nonpressured environment. Don't be intense or loud because that will turn him off. Use gentle, probing questions, and suggest that it's okay to think about his answers for a while before responding. And when he's ready to speak, listen attentively without interrupting.

Show interest in his solitary activities too.[24]

Praying for Your Kids

"What is the best way to pray for my children and me?"

Sometimes we can get so busy as parents that prayer is a last-minute thought or half-finished. Here are some practical ideas.

- Pray when you're fresh and alert. This time may vary because of your metabolism.

- When you pray, be specific.

- Have you prayed Scripture passages aloud? Take the promises of God's Word and use them as prayers for your children and yourself.

- Keep a prayer journal. Don't just list your requests, but also write out some of your prayers in detail. Our memories fade, especially when we get older. When a prayer is answered, go back to the request and write in the answer and the date.

- Ask God what He wants you to pray about for your children.

- Some of the prayers you pray for your children are "future" or "waiting" prayers.

Raising Responsible Adults

"How do we help our children stand on their own when they're adults?"

Here's what three grown children said about how their parents helped them grow up.

A daughter shared:

> My parents have made a lot of decisions for me and yet have made me make a lot of decisions. They have given me freedom when I've shown I can handle it responsibly.

A son shared:

> I know my parents have really cared about our lives and what we've been interested in. They haven't said, "Kids, we're going to do this because your father and I want you to do this," or anything like that. They consulted us about activities we wanted.

Another son said:

> You and Mom didn't let me do whatever I wanted, but you gave me freedom nonetheless.

Creating Good Ones

"What's the best way to set rules and limits with my children? I also teach and could use some help in class."

A rule should be definable. If it is well-defined, they will know instantly when they have broken it. It must be so specifically presented that everyone knows what the rule is all about. If you tell your daughter she can't go outside until her room is clean, that is a poorly defined rule. If you tell her to make the bed, empty the trash, and hang up her clothes on hangers, you are getting closer to a defined rule.

A rule should be reasonable. The rule should make the environment more comfortable for the children and those around them. Make sure it is a rule the children are capable of following.

A rule should be enforceable. Anticipate that rules may be broken. Most children like to test rules. If you can't or don't enforce a rule consistently, it's unrealistic to expect the children to follow it.

A rule should help develop inner values and control. The rule should help children eventually become independent, responsible people.

Teaching Children Respect

"My kids won't obey or respect me. What can I do?"

Consider a new approach: Listen to what they say. I've been impressed by a book by Buddy Scott called *Relief for Hurting Parents*. One of his concepts is that our children teach us what to do and how to respond by their actions. This may be a new thought to you. Here are some examples. Notice how the consequences fit the offense.

> Children *who teach us* that we cannot trust them out of our sight must remain in our sight (grounded and more closely supervised)...
>
> Children *who teach us* that we cannot trust what they say must understand that we'll be checking almost everything they say.
>
> Children *who teach us* that we cannot trust them to remain sober must no longer be allowed to drive the family car...
>
> Children *who teach us* that they will let their grades fall must be more closely supervised in their studying.[25]

Sex

Handling Awkward Questions

"My kids are starting to ask me about sex. I'm not sure I'm ready for that."

This is what most parents fear—especially the question, "Do you do it?" But today sex is everywhere. Your children will get an education and probably before you want them to. I recommend:

- Read books on sex and sexual behavior. You want to know more than your kids.
- Look for teachable moments. If they don't bring it up, you need to. Encourage questions frequently.
- Hold practice discussions with your spouse so both of you can get over any discomfort.
- Use proper terminology—penis, vagina, intercourse, semen, and so forth. Ask your kids what terms their friends use. Be ready to talk about AIDS, gays, transgender, oral sex, wet dreams.
- Read Scriptures together: homosexuality (Leviticus 18:22; Romans 1:26-27); incest (Leviticus 20:13; 1 Corinthians 5); rape (Deuteronomy 22:23-29). Sex is good in God's sight; sex for pleasure is OK (Genesis 1:26-28; 1 Timothy 4:4-5; Deuteronomy 24:5; Proverbs 5:18-20; Song of Solomon; Genesis 38:9-10).

Generous or Not?

"I want my kids to have everything they need or want. So what if they're spoiled a little?"

There is harm in spoiling a child.

1. *Indulged children expect their whims to be satisfied.* They never build a tolerance for frustration or learn to delay gratification.

2. *Children rarely feel fulfilled.* Any sense of satisfaction they may enjoy is momentary.

3. *Children become dependent on gifts* as tangible proof that they are loved.

4. *Children don't live harmoniously with other children.* They become selfish, self-centered, and self-indulgent.

5. *Children are ill-prepared to handle stress.*

6. *The families of indulged children don't develop real cohesiveness.* Children compete with each other to see who can get the most.

7. *Indulged children live in an "unreal" world.* Indulging parents create a home *environment* that is far removed from the real world.[26]

How to Be Supportive

"We're a sports family. We want our kids to excel. Any suggestions so it doesn't get out of hand?"

Today there is an enormous emphasis on excelling and winning. Few parents or coaches teach children how to handle frustration or defeat. There's little emphasis on character-building; instead, the teaching is more centered on egotism and aggression.[27]

You can help your children keep athletics in perspective by being encouraging but gentle and supportive. Emphasize the value of trying, improving, and having fun along the way.

Be careful not to over-praise.

Above all, remember whose game it is—your children's. Don't let your children's sports dominate your family life.

First, *don't question the calls*. Who are the coaches and referees, after all? They're people just like you.

Second, *don't analyze the game from a critical perspective*, especially in front of your child.

Too many parents teach their children to concentrate on the goal instead of experiencing the journey and life along the way.[28]

Preparing Children for Hard Choices

"What's the best way to help my kids handle difficult temptations and avoid adopting non-Christian values?"

You're in the doctor's office waiting with your child. Soon you're called into the examining room, where the doctor takes out a needle and carefully injects the contents into the arm of your wide-eyed child. While the shot may have hurt momentarily, it is of important and lasting consequence because your child was just inoculated against a life-threatening disease. In similar fashion, the best way to help them develop the character they need is to inoculate them against what they will encounter. How do you do this?

Don't keep your children in a protected, "hothouse" environment. This will weaken their resistance. Expose them gradually, bit by bit, to problems and stresses. While you're doing it, talk with them and show them how to handle what they're encountering. That way they're better prepared and not thrown off course.

Gradual exposure means giving your children responsibilities and not shielding them from the unpleasant situations of life. It requires being truthful even when your children can get hurt.